# In the Embrace
## A Journey Thro...

Celebrating your year
1979
A memorable year for

# TABLE OF CONTENTS

# TABLE OF CONTENTS

**6**

## TECHNOLOGY AND INNOVATION

**7**

## THE COST OF THINGS

**8**

## BIRTHS IN 1979

# Introduction

"1979 Chronicles: Chronicles of a Pivotal Historical Epoch"

Step into the tender embrace of 1979, a transformative year that echoes with the whispers of change, the resonance of monumental events, and the heartfelt rhythm of a world evolving. Whether you have witnessed its history unfold or are drawn to its enigmatic allure, this book serves as a heartfelt homage to the enduring legacy of a defining epoch.

Immerse yourself in the vivid tableau of cherished memories, evocative anecdotes, and pivotal moments that intricately compose the mosaic of 1979. Journey through the pages as they unveil the riveting narratives and profound sentiments that define the essence of this remarkable chapter in the annals of time.

Enjoy each chapter to envelop you in a tender embrace of nostalgia, igniting a fervent exploration and fostering an intimate connection to the captivating stories that continue to shape our collective narrative. Join us as we traverse the expanse of 1979, where the past beckons with its resounding tales, and the spirit of an era calls upon us to bask in its timeless narrative, forever etched in the tapestry of history.

Warmest regards,
Edward Art Lab

# Chapter 1: World Politics

*The year 1979 was marked by significant political events that had far-reaching consequences globally. Here's a brief overview of the major events*

# 1. Remarkable political events of '79

## UK -Public Sector workers strike

January 22nd, 1979: Public sector workers, organized by the four largest public sector unions, went on strike in response to the British government's decision to impose a five percent pay increase ceiling. The unions represented a substantial number of workers, totaling around one and a half million members.

The events of the Winter of Discontent ultimately contributed to the decline of the Labour government led by Prime Minister James Callaghan

## Margaret Thatcher became the UK's first female Prime Minister

Margaret Thatcher became the UK's first female Prime Minister, leading the Conservative Party. Her policies would later come to be known as Thatcherism, emphasizing free-market economics and a reduction in the role of the state.

## Iranian Transformation

Ayatollah Khomeini led the Iranian Revolution, toppling the monarchy and establishing an Islamic Republic. This event drastically transformed Iran's political and social landscape, leading to significant changes in the country's domestic and international policies.

## Cold War Parleys

The United States and the Soviet Union signed the SALT II Treaty (Strategic Arms Limitation Talks), a bilateral agreement aimed at curbing the arms race between the two superpowers. However, the treaty faced significant challenges and was never ratified by the United States Senate.

## The Fall of a Tyrant

Idi Amin, the notorious Ugandan dictator known for his brutal regime, was overthrown, ending his destructive rule characterized by human rights abuses and economic turmoil.

Pope John Paul II's visit to communist Poland held significant symbolic importance, inspiring the Polish people and contributing to the eventual collapse of communist rule in Eastern Europe.

## The Rise of Saddam

Saddam Hussein seized power and became the President of Iraq, later leading the country through a tumultuous period marked by the Iran-Iraq War, the Gulf War, and a series of internal conflicts.

## Troubles in Northern Ireland

In December 1979, the Soviet Union invaded Afghanistan in an attempt to prop up the pro-Soviet government in Kabul, which was facing a rising insurgency. The invasion marked a significant turning point in the Cold War and had far-reaching consequences for both Afghanistan and the global political landscape. The Soviet Union's military intervention triggered a long and devastating conflict that lasted nearly a decade.

## Nicaragua's Revolution

   The Sandinista National Liberation Front overthrew the Nicaraguan regime, leading to the establishment of a left-wing government and a period of political and social reforms in Nicaragua.

## 2. Major World Political Leaders in 1979

### Jimmy Carter

United States President Jimmy Carter: Carter is known for his advocacy for human rights and his efforts to advance peace negotiations in the Middle East, as well as for his emphasis on energy conservation and environmental protection.

## Margaret Thatcher

Thatcher is known for her conservative policies, which emphasized free-market economics, privatization, and a strong stance against trade unions. Her leadership had a profound impact on the UK's political and economic landscape.

## Leonid Brezhnev

As Soviet Union First Secretary of the CPSU, Brezhnev's leadership was characterized by a period of stability in the Soviet Union, marked by a focus on detente with the West and the expansion of Soviet influence in global affairs.

## Malcolm Fraser

Holding the position of Australia Prime Minister, Fraser is known for his conservative leadership during a tumultuous period in Australian politics, including significant economic challenges and social change.

## Helmut Schmidt

He was Germany's Chancellor. Schmidt's leadership in Germany was characterized by his commitment to European cooperation and his handling of economic challenges and political tensions during the Cold War era.

## Giulio Andreotti

As the Prime Minister of Italy, Andreotti is known for his long political career and his contributions to Italian politics and foreign policy during a challenging period in the country's history.

## Valéry Giscard d'Estaing

As President of France, Giscard d'Estaing is known for his modernization efforts and contributions to European integration, including the establishment of the European Council.

## Pieter Willem Botha

Served as the Prime Minister of South Africa, Botha is remembered for his role in implementing reforms in South Africa, including limited reforms to apartheid policies and attempts to address racial tensions.

# Activity: Historical Triava Quiz
# Test Your Knowledge of 1979

*Are you ready to challenge your knowledge of the significant events and key figures of 1979? Here's a historical trivia quiz to test your knowledge of the events and leaders in 1979:*

1. Who was the first female Prime Minister of the United Kingdom, elected in 1979?
a) Margaret Thatcher
b) Angela Merkel
c) Golda Meir
d) Indira Gandhi

2. What was the name of the revolutionary leader who overthrew the Somoza regime in Nicaragua in 1979?
a) Che Guevara
b) Fidel Castro
c) Augusto Sandino
d) Daniel Ortega

3. Which Soviet leader's death in 1979 marked the end of an era and paved the way for significant changes in the Soviet Union?
a) Nikita Khrushchev
b) Joseph Stalin
c) Mikhail Gorbachev
d) Leonid Brezhnev

4. What significant peace agreement was brokered by President Jimmy Carter in 1979, leading to the normalization of relations between Egypt and Israel?
a) Camp David Accords
b) Oslo Accords
c) Paris Peace Accords
d) Good Friday Agreement

5. Which country did the Soviet Union invade in December 1979, leading to a protracted and devastating conflict that lasted nearly a decade?
a) Afghanistan
b) Iraq
c) Iran
d) Vietnam

6. Who was the President of France in 1979, known for his modernization efforts and contributions to European integration?
a) François Mitterrand
b) Charles de Gaulle
c) Valéry Giscard d'Estaing
d) Jacques Chirac

7. Who was the Chancellor of West Germany in 1979, known for his contributions to economic stability and European cooperation?
a) Konrad Adenauer
b) Helmut Kohl
c) Willy Brandt
d) Helmut Schmidt

8. Which Indian Prime Minister, known for his advocacy of social and economic reforms, was in power in 1979?
a) Rajiv Gandhi
b) Indira Gandhi
c) Morarji Desai
d) Jawaharlal Nehru

# Chapter 2: Entertainment in 1979

# Films and Prestigious Film Awards

In 1979, cinema was undergoing a transition with the decline of the Golden Age of Hollywood and the rise of more independent, innovative filmmaking.

## 1. Memorable Films of '79

### Kramer vs. Kramer

Directed by Robert Benton, this critically acclaimed drama won five Academy Awards, including Best Picture and Best Actor for Dustin Hoffman. Meryl Streep also received an Oscar for Best Supporting Actress for her role in the film.

## The Amityville Horror

Based on Jay Anson's novel of the same name, this horror film tells the story of a haunted house in Amityville, New York. Despite receiving mixed reviews, the movie was a commercial success and has become a classic in the horror genre. "The Amityville Horror" received commercial success, becoming one of the highest-grossing independent films of its time

## Rocky II

This sequel to the original Rocky film follows the titular character, played by Sylvester Stallone, as he faces new challenges and adversaries in his boxing career. The movie further solidified the Rocky franchise's popularity and Stallone's career as an action star.

## Apocalypse Now

Directed by Francis Ford Coppola, this war film is regarded as one of the greatest movies ever made. Its portrayal of the Vietnam War is known for its intensity and visual storytelling, earning critical acclaim and numerous accolades.

## Star Trek

This film marked the beginning of the Star Trek movie franchise, continuing the adventures of the original Star Trek television series. Although it received mixed reviews upon release, it laid the groundwork for the enduring popularity of the Star Trek film series.

## Alien

Directed by Ridley Scott, this science fiction horror film introduced audiences to the terrifying xenomorph creature and the resilient protagonist Ellen Ripley, played by Sigourney Weaver. Alien received critical acclaim for its suspenseful plot, innovative special effects, and strong performances.

## 2. Prestigious Film Awards

Here are some key highlights from the major awards ceremonies that year

### Academy Awards (Oscars)

The 51st Academy Awards ceremony honored films released in 1978 and took place on April 9, 1979, in Los Angeles. :

**Best Picture:**
The Deer Hunter

**Best Director:**
Michael Cimino – The Deer Hunter

**Best Actor:**
Jon Voight – Coming Home

**Best Actress:**
Jane Fonda – Coming Home

# Golden Globe Awards

The 36th Golden Globe Awards, honoring the best in film and television for 1978, were held on January 27, 1979.

**Best Motion Picture - Drama:**
Midnight Express

**Best Motion Picture - Musical or Comedy:**
Heaven Can Wait

**Best Director:**
Michael Cimino – The Deer Hunter

**Best Actor - Drama:**
Jon Voight – Coming Home

**Best Actress - Drama:**
Jane Fonda – Coming Home

### Best Actor - Musical or Comedy:
Warren Beatty – Heaven Can Wait

### Best Actress - Musical or Comedy:
Ellen Burstyn – Same Time, Next Year
Maggie Smith – California Suite

*Ellen Burstyn*        Maggie Smith

## Cannes Film Festival

The 32nd Cannes Film Festival was held from 10 to 24 May 1979. The Palme d'Or went to **Apocalypse Now** by Francis Ford Coppola, which was screened as a work in progress, and **Die Blechtrommel** (The Tin Drum) by Volker Schlöndorff.

*Apocalypse Now by Francis Ford Coppola*

*Die Blechtrommel (The Tin Drum) by Volker Schlöndorff*

# Music: Top Songs and Awards

## 1. Top songs

### "My Sharona" by The Knack

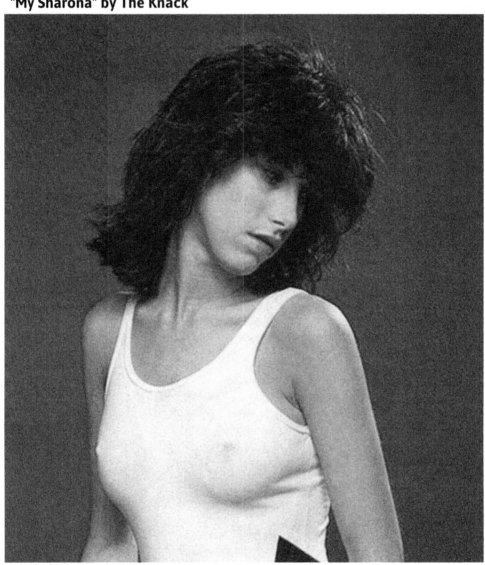

This power pop/rock song became a cultural phenomenon, topping the charts in various countries and showcasing The Knack's energetic sound. Its catchy melody and memorable guitar riff contributed to its enduring popularity and influence in the rock genre.

## "Bad Girls" by Donna Summer

Released as part of her album of the same name, "Bad Girls" showcased Summer's versatility as a disco and pop artist. The song's fusion of disco and rock elements, along with its empowering lyrics, solidified its place as a timeless anthem and a significant contribution to the disco genre.

## "Heart of Glass" by Blondie

Considered a pioneering track in the new wave and punk rock genres, "Heart of Glass" marked a shift in Blondie's sound towards more pop-oriented elements. Its fusion of disco and rock influences, along with Debbie Harry's distinctive vocals, helped the song achieve widespread acclaim and cultural significance.

### "I Will Survive" by Gloria Gaynor

This disco anthem became an empowering symbol of resilience and strength, resonating with audiences worldwide. Its uplifting message and infectious rhythm made it a timeless classic, solidifying its place as one of the most iconic disco songs of all time.

### "Le Freak" by Chic

With its infectious rhythm and funky disco vibes, "Le Freak" became a disco sensation, showcasing Chic's musical prowess and Nile Rodgers' exceptional guitar skills. The song's success and lasting influence contributed to its recognition as one of the most popular and enduring disco tracks in music history.

## "Y.M.C.A." by Village People

This disco hit became a global anthem for celebration and unity, renowned for its catchy chorus and danceable beats. Its enduring popularity and iconic status within the disco genre have solidified its place in popular culture and its influence on dance music and LGBTQ+ communities.

## "Don't Stop 'Til You Get Enough" by Michael Jackson

This funk and disco-infused track marked the beginning of Michael Jackson's successful solo career. Its infectious groove, captivating vocals, and innovative production set the stage for Jackson's future musical endeavors, cementing his status as a pop music icon and innovator.

## "Love You Inside Out" by the Bee Gees

Released in 1979 as part of their album "Spirits Having Flown." The track exemplifies the Bee Gees' signature disco sound, featuring catchy melodies, harmonious vocals, and a danceable beat. "Love You Inside Out" was well-received by audiences and critics, achieving commercial success and topping the charts in several countries, including the United States, Canada, and the United Kingdom.

## "Ring My Bell" by Anita Ward

"Ring My Bell" is known for its catchy chorus and upbeat, danceable melody, which contributed to its widespread popularity and enduring status as a disco classic. This song became one of the most successful disco singles of the late 1970s, showcasing Anita Ward's dynamic vocals and the infectious rhythm that defined the era.

## "Sad Eyes" by Robert John

"Sad Eyes" is a soft rock song, was a significant commercial success. "Sad Eyes" is characterized by its smooth, melodic sound and emotive lyrics, which reflect themes of heartbreak and longing.

## 2. Renowned singers and bands of '79

1979 saw the continued prominence of several renowned singers, each making significant contributions to the music industry. Some of the noteworthy singers during that period were:

**Donna Summer**

Often referred to as the "Queen of Disco," was one of the most influential and successful artists In 1979. Known for her powerful and soulful voice, she became a defining figure in the disco genre, leaving an indelible mark on popular music. Throughout 1979, Donna Summer continued to contribute to the vibrant musical landscape with her chart-topping hits "Bad Girls" and "Hot Stuff".

## Blondie

Fronted by the charismatic Debbie Harry, Blondie made a significant impact on the music scene with their blend of new wave and punk rock. Their chart-topping singles, including "Heart of Glass" and "Call Me," showcased their eclectic style and paved the way for their enduring influence in the realms of rock and pop music.

## Michael Jackson

The late 1970s marked a crucial turning point in Michael Jackson's career as he transitioned to solo stardom with the release of his groundbreaking album "Off the Wall." The album's hit singles, such as "Don't Stop 'Til You Get Enough" and "Rock with You," solidified Jackson's position as a pop music icon and set the stage for his unparalleled success in the following decades.

## The Eagles

As one of the most successful American rock bands in 1979, The Eagles continued to captivate audiences with their signature blend of country, rock, and folk. Their classic album "Hotel California" featured the eponymous hit single, further solidifying their status as pioneers of the West Coast rock sound.

## Commodores

Led by Lionel Richie, the Commodores made waves in the R&B and funk scene with their soulful ballads and infectious grooves. Tracks such as "Three Times a Lady" and "Still" showcased the group's exceptional vocal harmonies and contributed to their widespread acclaim and success.

## Pink Floyd

Known for their progressive and psychedelic rock sound, Pink Floyd released their monumental concept album "The Wall" in 1979. The album's narrative depth, combined with its innovative production and musical complexity, solidified Pink Floyd's reputation as one of the most influential and visionary rock bands in history.

## The Police

Fronted by Sting, The Police seamlessly blended elements of new wave, punk, and reggae, creating a distinctive sound that captivated audiences worldwide. Hit "Message in a Bottle" showcased the group's dynamic energy and exceptional musicianship, contributing to their significant impact on the music scene.

## Village People

With their infectious disco and dance-pop hits, Village People became synonymous with the vibrant disco era. Track "Y.M.C.A." not only dominated the charts but also became cultural touchstones, solidifying the group's legacy as pioneers of disco and dance music.

# Activity: Music Lyrics Challenge - Guess the Song Lyrics from '79

Test your knowledge of '79 music with this fun lyrics challenge!
See if you can match the lyrics to the songs mentioned in the chapter.

**Directions**: Match the given song lyrics from 1979 to their respective songs. Can you correctly identify which song each set of lyrics belongs to?

*Lyrics:*
1. "You know, I was
   I was wondering, you know..."

2. "Ooh, my little pretty one, pretty one..."

3. "Young man there's no need to feel down..."

4. "At first I was afraid, I was petrified"

5. "I'm glad you're home
   Now did you really miss me?"

**Songs:**
a. My Sharona
b. Don't Stop 'til You Get Enough
c. Ring My Bell
d. Y.M.C.A.
e. I Will Survive

# Chapter 3:
# Art and Literature
# in 1979

In the realm of art and literature, 1979 was marked by a variety of notable achievements and contributions. Some significant events and works from that year:

## Popular books published in 1979

### 1. "The Hitchhiker's Guide to the Galaxy" by Douglas Adams

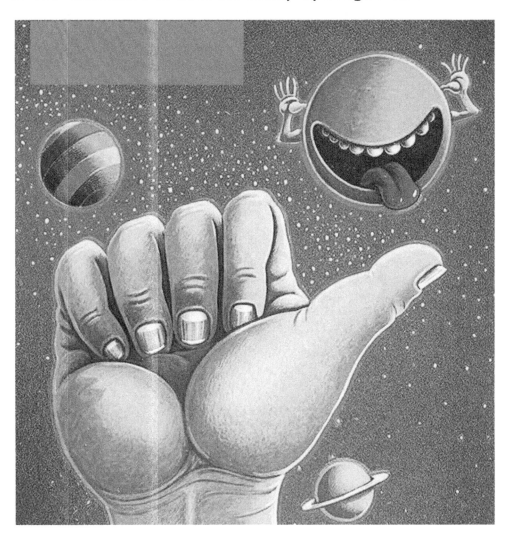

This comedic science fiction novel, which originated from a BBC radio comedy, became a cult classic, captivating readers with its witty and satirical exploration of the universe.

## 2. "Sophie's Choice" by William Styron

A powerful and haunting novel that delves into the complexities of human relationships and the lasting impact of World War II, "Sophie's Choice" earned critical acclaim for its poignant narrative and exploration of profound themes.

## 3. "If On a Winter's Night a Traveler" by Italo Calvino

This postmodern novel, known for its experimental narrative structure and playful exploration of storytelling, captivated readers with its inventive and thought-provoking approach to literature. It has garnered critical acclaim for its intellectual richness and its inventive approach to examining the art of storytelling, establishing Italo Calvino as a prominent figure in postmodern literature.

## 4. "The Dead Zone" by Stephen King

Stephen King's gripping psychological thriller, "The Dead Zone," explores themes of fate, second chances, and the consequences of extraordinary abilities. The novel's suspenseful plot and well-drawn characters solidified King's reputation as a master of the horror and thriller genres.

## 5. "Kindred" by Octavia Butler

A groundbreaking work of speculative fiction, "Kindred" follows the story of a contemporary African American woman who is mysteriously transported back in time to the antebellum South. Octavia Butler's powerful narrative addresses themes of race, history, and identity, making it a significant contribution to the genre of Afrofuturism.

## 6. The New Drawing on the Right Side of the Brain

"The New Drawing on the Right Side of the Brain" is a highly influential and widely popular instructional book on drawing, authored by Betty Edwards. First published in 1979, the book presents a unique approach to drawing that emphasizes the importance of tapping into the creative and intuitive right hemisphere of the brain.

**Its holistic and accessible approach to drawing has made it a timeless resource, influencing generations of artists and learners and solidifying its reputation as a seminal work in the field of art education.**

# Arts in 1979

The year 1979 was marked by various artistic movements and cultural developments that left a lasting impact on the world of arts.

### Archibald Prize
 Wes Walters  won the Archibald Prize in 1979 for his portrait of Phillip Adams

## Influential figures in the arts in 1979

**Emerging Street Art:** 1979 saw the rise of street art as a prominent form of artistic expression. Artists such as Keith Haring and Jean-Michel Basquiat began to gain recognition for their vibrant and dynamic graffiti-inspired works, contributing to the flourishing street art movement that would later have a profound influence on contemporary art and culture.

## Postmodernism in Visual Art

The principles of postmodernism continued to make an impact on the visual arts during this period, challenging traditional norms and exploring new conceptual territories. Artists experimented with diverse mediums and conceptual approaches, leading to a proliferation of diverse and unconventional artistic expressions.

*New York School of Visual Arts 1979*

## Feminist Art Movement

The feminist art movement continued to make strides in challenging gender norms and addressing social and political issues through various artistic mediums. Artists like Judy Chicago and Cindy Sherman used their work to critique and confront societal expectations, contributing to a growing awareness of gender equality and representation within the art world.

### The Dinner Party, Judy Chicago, Mixed media, 1979.
Widely regarded as the first epic feminist artwork, it offers a symbolic history of women in Western civilization

## Sculptures

Lee Kelly is one of the prominent American sculptors known for his abstract and geometric sculptures. His works are characterized by a harmonious integration with the natural environment and an exploration of form and space.

*Lee Kelly's sculpture Nash in Portland*

# Activity: Search puzzle related to Literature and Art in 1979

Are your ready to challenge your knowledge of literature and art in 1979?

## Literature and Art in 1979

Y K O G A C I H C Y D U J L
T O W E S W A L T E R S W B
R O N D Y B D B D D A T D E
A B S S S U S F E E H H G T
P K A I T T Y E E V L E W T
R E R I R T I M E U K D D Y
E T F L E R R I T L I E D E
N L O E E A E N E H N A S D
N D C E T L D I T S D D A W
I D D K A A D S R N R Z O A
D R R E R U W T S T E O I R
E S E L T S L A H E D N I D
H O H L T I B R I T I E E S
T W S Y E V L T N N K C W T

LEE KELLY
BOOK
BETTY EDWARDS
KINDRED
THE DINNER PARTY

VISUAL ART
FEMINIST ART
JUDY CHICAGO
WES WALTERS
THE DEAD ZONE
STREET ART

**Enjoy solving the crossword puzzle!**

# Chapter 4:
# Sports in 1979
# A Journey
# Through the World

In 1979, the world of sports witnessed various significant events and achievements across different athletic disciplines. Some of the notable occurrences in the realm of sports

## Football

Super Bowl XIII, held on January 21, 1979, was won by the Pittsburgh Steelers of the American Football Conference (AFC), who defeated the Dallas Cowboys of the National Football Conference (NFC) with a score of 35 to 31. This victory marked the Steelers' third Super Bowl win in the span of five years, solidifying their status as one of the dominant teams of the era.

## Baseball

The Pittsburgh Pirates claimed the World Series championship in 1979, triumphing over the Baltimore Orioles in a closely contested seven-game series. The season was characterized by remarkable performances and memorable moments

## Basketball

In 1979, the Seattle SuperSonics, led by coach Lenny Wilkens, clinched the NBA Finals championship by defeating the Washington Bullets with a 4-1 series win. This victory marked the only NBA Finals win in the history of the Seattle SuperSonics franchise, showcasing the team's exceptional skill and determination throughout the season.

## Golf

Fuzzy Zoeller claimed victory at the Masters Tournament. Hale Irwin emerged as the champion of the U.S and Seve Ballesteros secured a memorable win at the British Open in 1979.

Hale Irwin won U.S. Open

Seve Ballesteros won The British Open

Fuzzy Zoeller won the Masters Tournament

## Ice Hockey

**Stanley Cup**: The Montreal Canadiens secured the Stanley Cup by defeating the New York Rangers in a series that concluded with a 4-1 victory.

**World Hockey Championship (Men's)**:
The Soviet Union clinched the World Hockey Championship title by defeating Czechoslovakia

# Horse racing

## Cheltenham Gold Cup

The Cheltenham Gold Cup in 1979 was won by the horse Alverton, showcasing its exceptional speed and endurance on the renowned Cheltenham Racecourse.

## Grand National

The Grand National of 1979 was claimed by the horse Rubstic, triumphing in the iconic steeplechase event held at the Aintree Racecourse. Rubstic's victory demonstrated its remarkable agility and skill over challenging steeplechase obstacles, solidifying its place in the history of the Grand National.

## Boxing

On September 28 in Las Vegas, Larry Holmes defended his World Heavyweight title by securing an 11th-round technical knockout (TKO) victory over Earnie Shavers. This win solidified Holmes' standing as a formidable heavyweight champion in the boxing world.

On November 30, also in Las Vegas, a dual world championship undercard unfolded. Vito Antuofermo retained his world Middleweight title following a grueling 15-round draw (tie) against the legendary Marvin Hagler. In the same event, Sugar Ray Leonard secured his first world title, triumphing over WBC world Welterweight champion Wilfred Benítez with a knockout in the 15th round. These bouts showcased the prowess and determination of these renowned boxers, captivating audiences and leaving an indelible mark on the sport of boxing.

*Vito Antuofermo*

*Sugar Ray Leonard*

# Tennis

## The Wimbledon Championships:

Björn Borg won in
the men's singles

Martina Navratilova won in
the women's singles

## The French Open:

Björn Borg won
in the men's singles

Chris Evert won
in the women's singles

## The US Open:

John McEnroe in
The men's singles

Tracy Austin in
in the women's singles

# Activity: Test Your Knowledge of 1979 Sports History

*Enjoy the multiple-choice quiz and see how well you remember the exciting sports history of 1979!*

1. Which team secured the World Series title in 1979?
a) Pittsburgh Pirates
b) Baltimore Orioles
c) New York Yankees
d) Los Angeles Dodgers

2. Who emerged as the winner of the NBA Finals in 1979?
a) Seattle SuperSonics
b) Washington Bullets
c) Boston Celtics
d) Los Angeles Lakers

3. Which golfer claimed victory at the Masters Tournament in 1979?
a) Jack Nicklaus
b) Arnold Palmer
c) Fuzzy Zoeller
d) Gary Player

4. Who won the U.S. Open in 1979?
a) Hale Irwin
b) Tiger Woods
c) Phil Mickelson
d) Jack Nicklaus

5. In which sport did Larry Holmes secure a notable victory in September 1979?
a) Tennis
b) Boxing
c) Wrestling
d) Mixed Martial Arts

6. Who emerged as the champion in the World Hockey Championship (Men's) in 1979?
a) Soviet Union
b) Canada
c) United States
d) Sweden

7. Which horse won the Cheltenham Gold Cup in 1979?
a) Kauto Star
b) Dawn Run
c) Desert Orchid
d) Alverton

# Chapter 5:
# Fashion, and Popular Leisure Activities

# Fashion

*Both women's and men's fashion in 1979 showcased a diverse range of styles, from the casual and comfortable to the more polished and sophisticated, capturing the essence of the late 1970s fashion landscape.*

## Women's fashion

**Denim Overalls**: Casual and comfortable denim overalls were a popular choice for women, reflecting the laid-back fashion of the late 1970s.

## Blouses with Bow Ties:

Blouses featuring bow ties were a fashionable trend, adding a touch of femininity to women's outfits.

**Wrap Dresses:** Inspired by the designs of Diane von Fürstenberg, wrap dresses gained popularity for their flattering silhouette and versatility.

**High-Waisted Jeans:** High-waisted jeans were in vogue, often paired with tucked-in blouses or shirts for a stylish look.

## Accessories

In 1979, knee-high and ankle boots were popular, often with a slouchy or chunky heel design. Heeled sandals, featuring open-toe styles and chunky heels, were also fashionable, reflecting the bold and eclectic trends of the late 1970s.

*Handbag in 1979*

*flip-top watch*

## Fashion for Men in 1979

**Blazers and Slacks:** Men's fashion embraced a more polished look with blazers, vests, and slacks, reflecting a blend of sophistication and casual elegance.

**Men's Cardigan Jackets:** were a popular outerwear choice, often worn over T-shirts or casual shirts for a relaxed yet stylish appearance.

**Corduroy Pants:** Corduroy pants, available in various colors, were a fashionable choice for men, providing both comfort and style.

# Popular Leisure Activities

**Hobbies**: toys were popular hobbies. The Speak & Spell toy was introduced by Texas Instruments in 1978, and it continued to be popular in 1979.

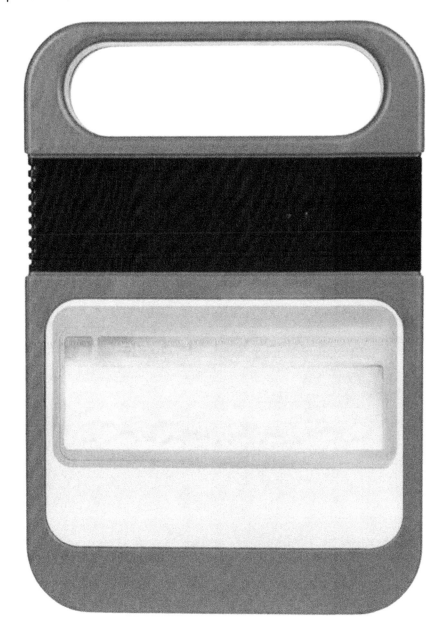

# Activity: Let's draw a picture of "fashion of 1979"

**Enjoy your artistic exploration of the fashion of 1979!**

# Chapter 6: Technological Advancements and Innovation

# Technological events

In 1979, several technological advancements and innovations contributed to the rapidly evolving landscape of science and technology. Some notable developments from that year:

## VisiCalc

The first electronic spreadsheet program, VisiCalc, was invented by Dan Bricklin and Bob Frankston in the United States. Its introduction revolutionized data processing and analysis, leading to the widespread use of electronic spreadsheets in various industries.

## Sony Walkman

Sony, a Japanese multinational company, introduced the groundbreaking Sony Walkman, which transformed the way people listened to music by offering a portable and personal audio experience. The Walkman quickly became a cultural icon, influencing the development of subsequent portable music devices.

## Voyager I's Photo of Jupiter's Rings

The Voyager I spacecraft, a part of NASA's Voyager program, captured and transmitted the first detailed images of Jupiter's rings. This technological achievement provided scientists with valuable insights into the composition and structure of Jupiter's planetary system.

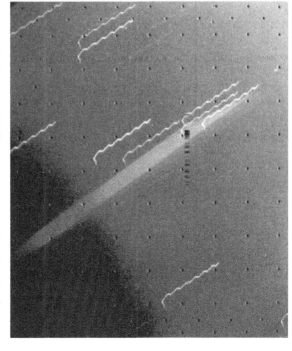

## Ariane 1 Launch

The European Space Agency (ESA) launched the Ariane 1, marking a significant milestone in Europe's space exploration efforts. The Ariane 1 launch vehicle played a crucial role in establishing Europe's presence in the competitive field of space technology and exploration.

## Snowboard

The modern snowboard, as we know it today, was invented by Sherman Poppen in the United States. His invention laid the foundation for the popular winter sport, providing enthusiasts with a thrilling and dynamic recreational activity.

## First Commercial Cellular Network

Nippon Telegraph and Telephone (NTT) in Japan established the first commercial cellular network, a groundbreaking development that laid the groundwork for modern cellular communication and the widespread adoption of mobile phones worldwide.

# The Automobiles of 1979

*In 1979, the automobile industry saw the introduction of several notable car models, with various manufacturers showcasing innovative designs and technological advancements.*

- **Dodge St. Regis**

The Dodge St. Regis was a full-size sedan that emphasized comfort and smooth driving, catering to the needs of consumers looking for a spacious and reliable vehicle.

- **Ford Durango**

The Ford Durango, a limited edition version of the Ford F-150, was designed as a sporty and rugged pickup truck, catering to consumers seeking versatility and performance.

- **Peugeot 505**

The Peugeot 505, known for its durability and comfortable ride, was a popular choice among consumers seeking a well-rounded and reliable mid-size car.

- **Mercedes-Benz W126**

The Mercedes-Benz W126 series, including the 280, 380, 500, and 300SD models, exemplified the brand's commitment to luxury, safety, and high-performance engineering, setting new standards in the luxury automobile market.

- ## Volkswagen Jetta

The Volkswagen Jetta, introduced as a compact sedan, combined practicality with a sporty design, offering consumers a reliable and fuel-efficient option in the compact car segment.

- **Lancia Delta**

The Lancia Delta, introduced as a compact hatchback, showcased the brand's commitment to stylish design and innovative engineering, appealing to consumers looking for a blend of performance and sophistication.

- **Dodge Omni 024**

The Dodge Omni 024, a subcompact hatchback, emphasized affordability and practicality, catering to consumers seeking an economical and reliable daily driving option.

# Activity: Test Your Knowledge of Technology in 1979

*"Welcome to the Milestone Fill-in activity! In this engaging challenge, you'll have the opportunity to fill in Technological events in the blank.*

1. The Sony Walkman was introduced in 1979, revolutionizing the way people listened to _____.

2. The European Space Agency launched the _____ in 1979, marking a significant milestone in Europe's space exploration efforts.

3. The first electronic spreadsheet program, VisiCalc, was developed in 1979, transforming data processing and analysis and paving the way for modern _____ software.

4. Nippon Telegraph and Telephone (NTT) established the first commercial _____ network in 1979, playing a pivotal role in shaping modern telecommunications.

5. The modern snowboard, as we know it today, was invented by _____ in the United States, contributing to the development of a popular winter sport.

# Chapter 7: The Cost of Things

## HOW MUCH YOU SPEND IN 1979

# Cost of Living in 1979

## United States:

- Average Cost of new house $58,100.00
- Average Income per year $17,500.00
- Average Monthly Rent $280.00
- Cost of a gallon of Gas 86 cents

## Cost of Living in 1979

- Sony Walkman $200.00
- Chess Challenger Computer Chess Game $199.49
- Pachinko Pinball Machine $199.49
- Jox Trainers $14.99
- Girls Denim Overalls $24.00
- Atari Video Computer System $199.00
- JVC VHS Video Recorder System $54.99
- Mens Blazer, Vest and Slacks $39.99
- King Size Bean Bag Chair $19.99
- Toyota Corola $3,698.00
- Mercury Couger XR7 $6,430.00

# Cost of Living in 1979

## United Kingdom:

- *Average House Price: £13,650*
- *Gallon of Petrol: £0.79*
- *Yearly Inflation Rate UK: 17.00%*
- *Interest Rates Year End Bank of England*

# Activity: How the life changed

Write your cost of living monthly

## SHOPPING LIST

- ☐
- ☐
- ☐
- ☐
- ☐
- ☐
- ☐
- ☐
- ☐
- ☐
- ☐
- ☐
- ☐
- ☐
- ☐
- ☐
- ☐

- ☐
- ☐
- ☐
- ☐
- ☐
- ☐
- ☐
- ☐
- ☐
- ☐
- ☐
- ☐
- ☐
- ☐
- ☐
- ☐
- ☐

# Activity: How the life changed

*Comparing prices from 1979 with the cost of similar items in the present day. Reflect on the changes in consumer behavior*

_____

_____

_____

_____

_____

_____

_____

_____

_____

_____

_____

_____

_____

_____

_____

_____

_____

_____

# Chapter 8:

# Births in 1979

*Several notable individuals were born in 1979 across various fields. Here are some famous births from that year:*

## 1. Kate Hudson

- Date of Birth: April 9th

The American actress gained acclaim for her roles in films such as "Almost Famous" and "Bride Wars," showcasing her talent and versatility in the entertainment industry. Throughout her career, Kate Hudson has demonstrated her ability to embody diverse and compelling characters, earning her a place among the celebrated actors of her generation.

## 2. Heath Ledger

- Date of Birth: April 4th

The Australian actor captivated audiences with his powerful performances in "Brokeback Mountain" and "The Dark Knight," posthumously winning an Academy Award for his unforgettable portrayal of the Joker. Heath Ledger's contribution to cinema is remembered not only for his remarkable talent but also for the depth and authenticity he brought to his roles.

## 3. Jennifer Love Hewitt

- Date of Birth: February 21st

The American actress and singer made significant contributions to television and film, notably through her roles in "Party of Five" and "Ghost Whisperer," solidifying her status as a prominent figure in the entertainment world. Jennifer Love Hewitt's career has spanned decades, making her a recognizable and respected figure in the entertainment industry.

## 4. Chris Pratt

- Date of Birth: June 21st

The American actor achieved widespread recognition for his roles in "Parks and Recreation," the "Guardians of the Galaxy" series, and "Jurassic World," establishing himself as a versatile and charismatic presence in Hollywood.

## 5. Pink

- Date of Birth: September 8th

Pink, whose real name is Alecia Beth Moore, is indeed a highly influential and accomplished American singer-songwriter. Known for her powerful and distinctive voice, she has made a significant impact on the music industry, particularly in the pop and rock genres. Pink's career took off in the late 1990s, and she has since released numerous chart-topping albums and hit singles. Some of her well-known songs include "Get the Party Started," "Just Like a Pill," "So What," and "Raise Your Glass." Her music often combines elements of pop, rock, and R&B, showcasing her versatility as an artist.

## 6. Kourtney Kardashian

- Date of Birth: April 18th

Kourtney Kardashian is a prominent American media personality, socialite, and businesswoman. The American media personality and businesswoman gained prominence through her appearances on the reality television series "Keeping Up with the Kardashians," contributing to her family's widespread influence in popular culture.

## 7. Tatyana Ali

- Date of Birth: January 24th

The American actress and singer gained recognition for her role as Ashley Banks in the iconic television series "The Fresh Prince of Bel-Air," contributing to the show's enduring popularity and cultural impact.

## 8. Kevin Hart

- Date of Birth: July 6th

**The American comedian and actor rose to prominence with his stand-up comedy specials and roles in hit films such as "Ride Along" and "Central Intelligence," solidifying his status as one of the leading comedians in the entertainment industry.**

# Activity: "Profiles in Achievement: The Noteworthy Births of 1979"

*Let's check your knowledge of famous births of 1979. Choose the correct answer (a, b, c, d) for each question.*

1. When was Kate Hudson born?
a) April 19th, 1979
b) August 12th, 1979
c) May 17th, 1979
d) July 6th, 1979

2. In which movie did Kate Hudson portray Penny Lane?
a) Almost Famous
b) How to Lose a Guy in 10 Days
c) Bride Wars
d) You, Me and Dupree

3. What character did Heath Ledger portray in "Brokeback Mountain"?
a) Jack Twist
b) Ennis Del Mar
c) Laramie Seymour Sullivan
d) Bobby Garfield

4. Which film showcased Jennifer Love Hewitt's role as Julie James?
a) I Know What You Did Last Summer
b) Heartbreakers
c) Can't Hardly Wait
d) Garfield: The Movie

5. What is Tatyana Ali's birthdate?
a) January 24th, 1979
b) August 21st, 1979
c) June 5th, 1979
d) October 12th, 1979


6. When was Jennifer Love Hewitt born?
a) February 21st, 1979
b) June 8th, 1982
c) March 14th, 1976
d) September 3rd, 1980

7. Which famous American singer was born on July 6th, 1979?
a) Kevin Hart
b) Tatyana Ali
c) 50 Cent
d) Kevin Federline

# Do you know Celebrities Born in 1979?

_____

_____

_____

_____

_____

_____

_____

_____

_____

_____

_____

_____

_____

_____

_____

_____

_____

_____

_____

# We have heartfelt thank-you gifts for you

As a token of our appreciation for joining us on this historical journey through 1979, we've included a set of cards and stamps inspired by the year of 1979. These cards are your canvas to capture the essence of the past. We encourage you to use them as inspiration for creating your own unique cards, sharing your perspective on the historical moments we've explored in this book. Whether it's a holiday greeting or a simple hello to a loved one, these cards are your way to connect with the history we've uncovered together.

**Happy creating!**

## Activity answers

### Chapter 1

1. C) Harold Wilson
2. B) Richard Nixon
3. A) The Apollo 11 moon landing
4. C) SALT I treaty
5. A) Georges Pompidou
6. D) Amnesty International
7. A) Pierre Trudeau
8. A) Vietnamization

### Chapter 2

1. b
2. a
3. d
4. e
5. c

### Chapter 3

```
Y K O G A C I H C Y D U J L
T O W E S W A L T E R S W B
R O N D Y B D B D D A T D E
A B S S S U S F E E H H G T
P K A I T T Y E E V L E W T
R E R I R T I M E U K D D Y
E T F L E R R I T L I E D E
N L O E E A E N E H N A S D
N D C E T L D I T S D D A W
I D D K A A D S R N R Z O A
D R R E R U W T S T E O I R
E S E L T S L A H E D N I D
H O H L T I B R I T I E E S
T W S Y E V L T N N K C W T
```

LEE KELLY
BOOK
BETTY EDWARDS
KINDRED
THE DINNER PARTY
VISUAL ART
FEMINIST ART
JUDY CHICAGO
WES WALTERS
THE DEAD ZONE
STREET ART

**Chapter 4:**
1. a) Pittsburgh Pirates
2. a) Seattle SuperSonics
3. c) Fuzzy Zoeller
4. a) Hale Irwin
5. b) Boxing
6. a) Soviet Union
7. d) Alverton

**Chapter 6:**
1. music
2. Ariane 1
3. spreadsheet
4. cellular
5. Sherman Poppen

**Chapter 8:**
1. a) April 19th, 1979
2. a) Almost Famous
3. b) Ennis Del Mar
4. a) I Know What You Did Last Summer
5. a) January 24th, 1979
6. a) February 21st, 1979
7. a) Kevin Hart

# Embracing 1979: A Grateful Farewell

Step into 1979: A Tapestry Woven with Triumphs and Transformations

Embark on a journey into the vibrant and dynamic landscape of 1979, a year that resonates with significant historical events and cultural shifts. Join us as we unravel the stories that have shaped the course of history, blending innovation with the spirit of progress.

Capturing Moments, Celebrating Achievements.

Your presence enriches the narrative of 1979, contributing valuable perspectives to the unfolding saga. Your insights form an integral part of preserving the essence of this pivotal year. Together, let's celebrate the milestones and ensure that the legacy of '79 remains a beacon for future generations.

We extend our heartfelt gratitude for your involvement in this extraordinary chapter of history. May the energy of '79 continue to kindle a passion for exploration, creativity, and societal advancement for generations to come.

# To Do List

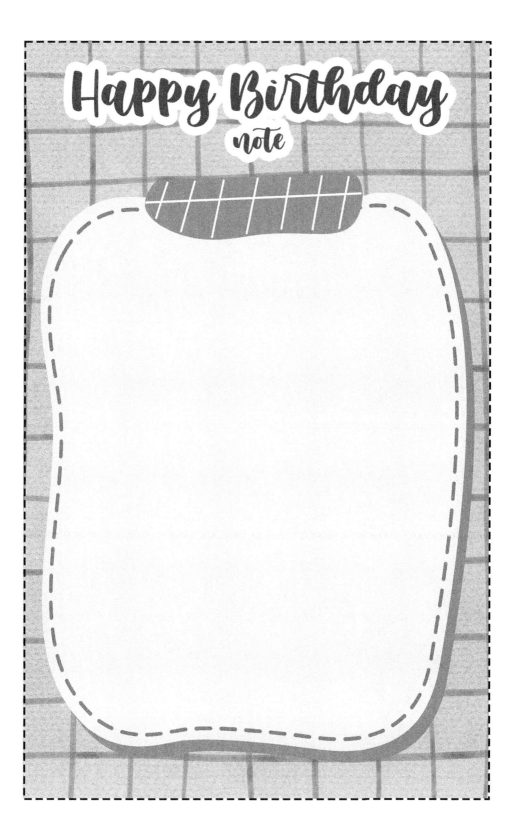

# Happy Birthday
### note

# Happy Birthday

note

# TO DO LIST

Name: _____    Day: _____    Month: _____

| No | To Do List | Yes | No |
|----|------------|-----|-----|
|    |            |     |     |
|    |            |     |     |
|    |            |     |     |
|    |            |     |     |
|    |            |     |     |
|    |            |     |     |
|    |            |     |     |
|    |            |     |     |
|    |            |     |     |
|    |            |     |     |
|    |            |     |     |
|    |            |     |     |
|    |            |     |     |

# TO DO LIST

Name: _____     Day: _____     Month: _____

| No | To Do List | Yes | No |
|----|------------|-----|----|
|    |            |     |    |
|    |            |     |    |
|    |            |     |    |
|    |            |     |    |
|    |            |     |    |
|    |            |     |    |
|    |            |     |    |
|    |            |     |    |
|    |            |     |    |
|    |            |     |    |
|    |            |     |    |
|    |            |     |    |
|    |            |     |    |

# NOTE

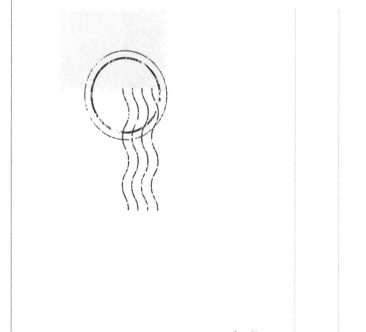

WISH YOU WERE HERE,
123 ANYWHERE ST., ANY CITY

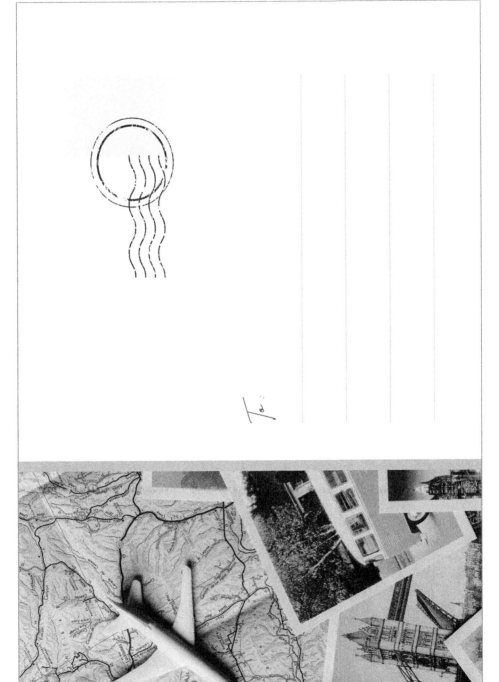

# HAPPY BIRTHDAY NOTE

# TO DO LIST

Name: _____  Day: _____  Month: _____

| No | To Do List | Yes | No |
|----|------------|-----|-----|
|    |            |     |     |
|    |            |     |     |
|    |            |     |     |
|    |            |     |     |
|    |            |     |     |
|    |            |     |     |
|    |            |     |     |
|    |            |     |     |
|    |            |     |     |
|    |            |     |     |
|    |            |     |     |
|    |            |     |     |
|    |            |     |     |

Remember This!

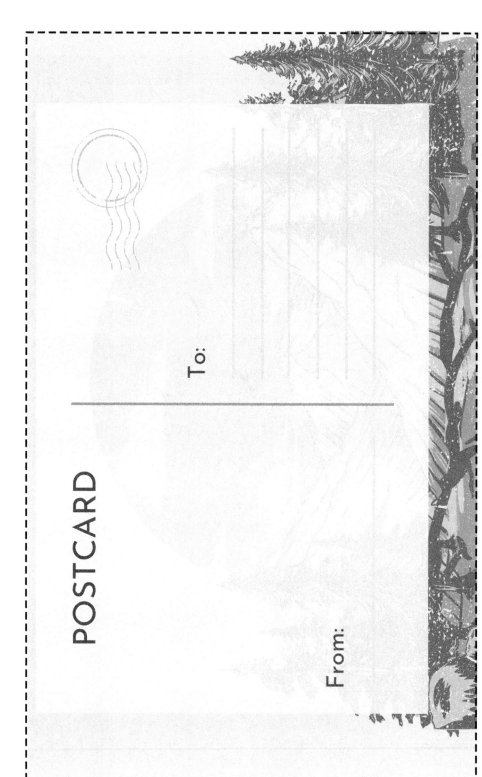

POSTCARD

To:

From:

Printed in Great Britain
by Amazon

34596199R00069